AF449061

# GEOGRAPHY FOR KIDS

## PATTERNS, LOCATION AND INTERRELATIONSHIPS

### THE WORLD IN SPATIAL TERMS

3rd Grade Social Studies

In this book, we're going to talk all about geography. So, let's get right to it!
N
W
E
S

# WHAT IS GEOGRAPHY?

Geography is the study of the physical features of planet Earth. It's also the study of how human beings influence the environment and how it influences them. There are three important questions that relate to the study of geography:

- How do people use Earth's resources?

- How do people interact with their environment, including living and nonliving things?

How does the Earth's land, air, water, and soil influence the way people live?

# PHYSICAL GEOGRAPHY VERSUS CULTURAL GEOGRAPHY

When geographers research a location, they may take a small region, such as a town, or they may research an entire country. Sometimes their studies focus on the whole world.

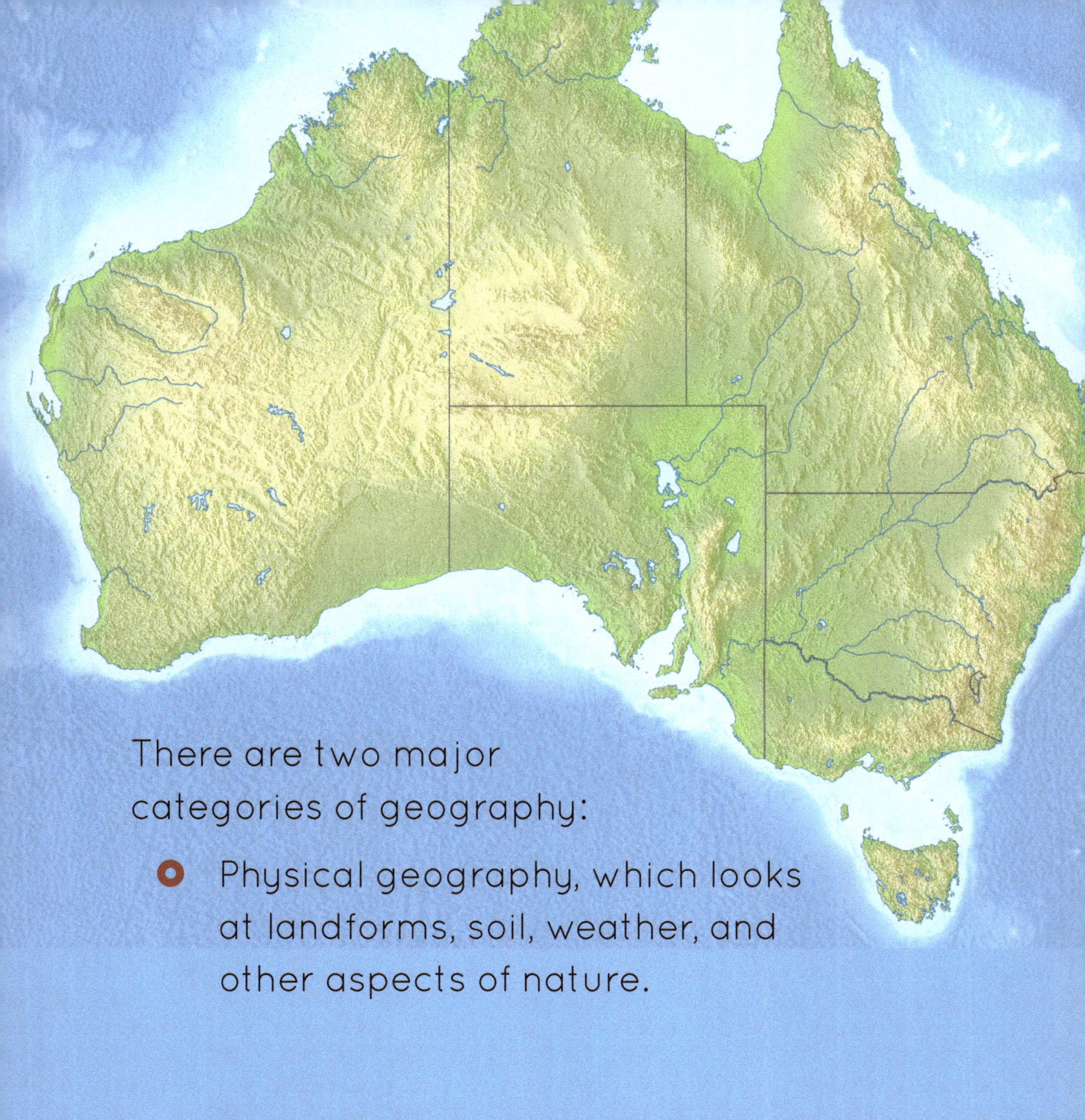

There are two major
categories of geography:

- Physical geography, which looks
  at landforms, soil, weather, and
  other aspects of nature.

- Cultural geography, which looks at how human beings interact with each other as well as their environment.

When people inhabit an area, they use the area's natural resources. They shape their environment by farming and building. They also use the cultural resources by working together to pool their creativity, practical skills, and knowledge.

COLORED SAND ART,
ORIGINATING IN CEARÁ

# GEOGRAPHY TOOLS

Geographers use maps and globes to help them define areas they want to study. Both of these types of tools are very useful, but they have disadvantages as well. A globe is a spherical model of the Earth. Because it's shaped like the Earth is actually shaped in reality, it shows the major landmasses and waterways accurately in relationship to each other.

0
30
60
N
NE
E
SE
S
APAN
Lhasa
ARU
BHUTAN
Bomdila
IMPHU
Tezpu
ASSAM  Naga
Guwahati  DISPUR
SHILONG
MEGHALAYA
Sylhet
BANGLADESH
AGARTALA
DHAKA
TRIPURA
WEST BENGAL

## PHYSICAL MAP OF AFRICA

On the other hand, maps take a portion of the Earth's surface, which is curved, and represent it as a flat drawing. Because of this, no flat map can show landmasses or waterways in accurate detail. In fact, the larger the region of the world a map depicts, the more inaccurate its relative sizes will be. If you compare the way the country of Greenland and the continent of Australia look on both a globe and a map, you'll see the type of distortion that occurs on a map.

espite this problem, maps are still very useful since they can show small regions with lots of details. There's no way that you could carry around a globe that would show all the details of cities or highways!

# PHYSICAL MAP OF EUROPE

# LATITUDE AND LONGITUDE

In order to divide physical maps into areas for study, geographers created a system that works like a grid. They use a system of imaginary lines to identify specific locations on Earth. A map is divided by these horizontal and vertical lines. Using these lines, which are called latitude and longitude, in tandem with the directions of north and south as well as east and west, you can pinpoint locations on Earth.

The top of the Earth is the North Pole and the South Pole is located at its bottom. The equator runs around the center of the Earth at its widest diameter.

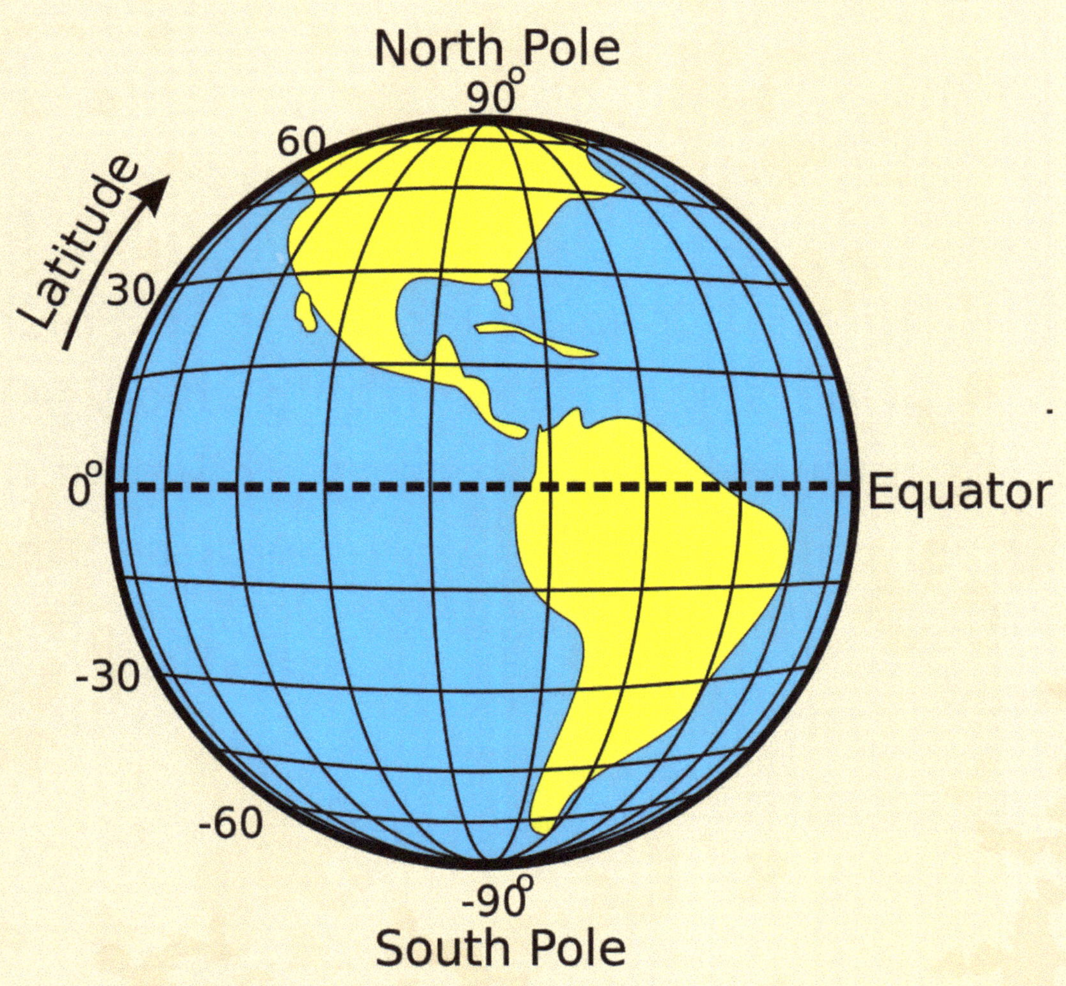

It is halfway between the North and South Poles. Everything north of the equator is in the Northern half or hemisphere of the Earth and everything south of the equator is in the Southern half or hemisphere of the Earth.

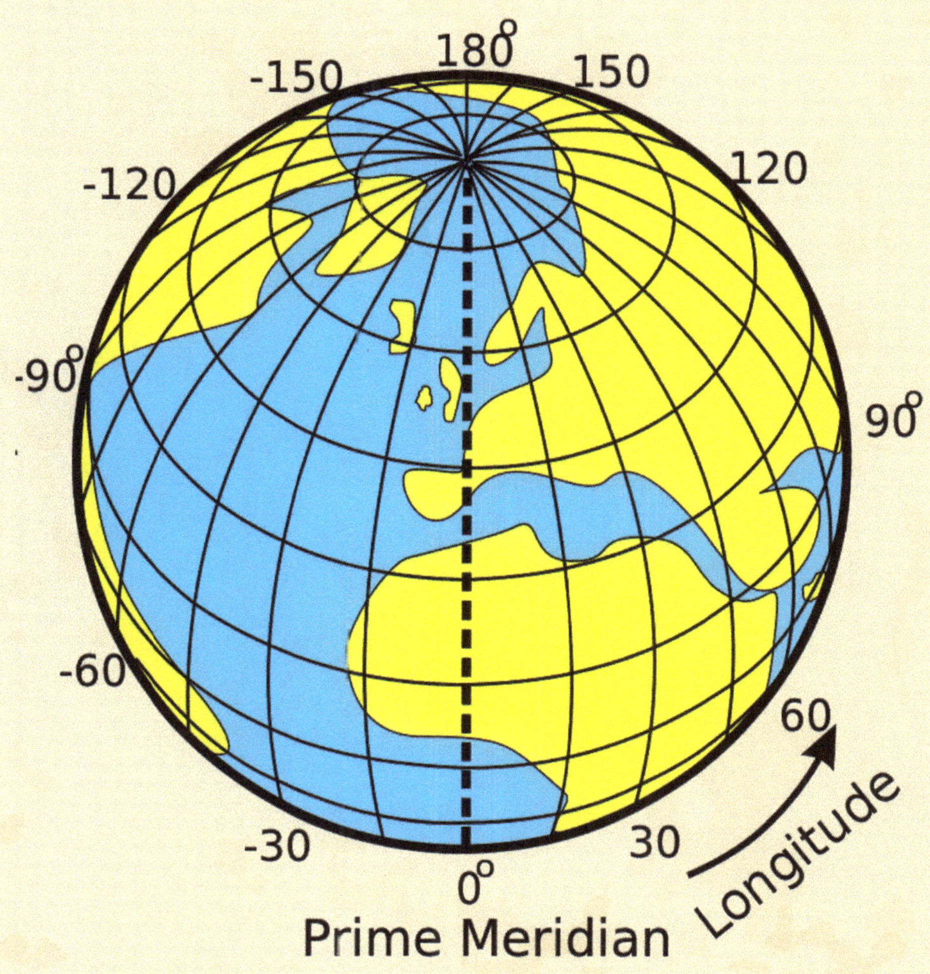

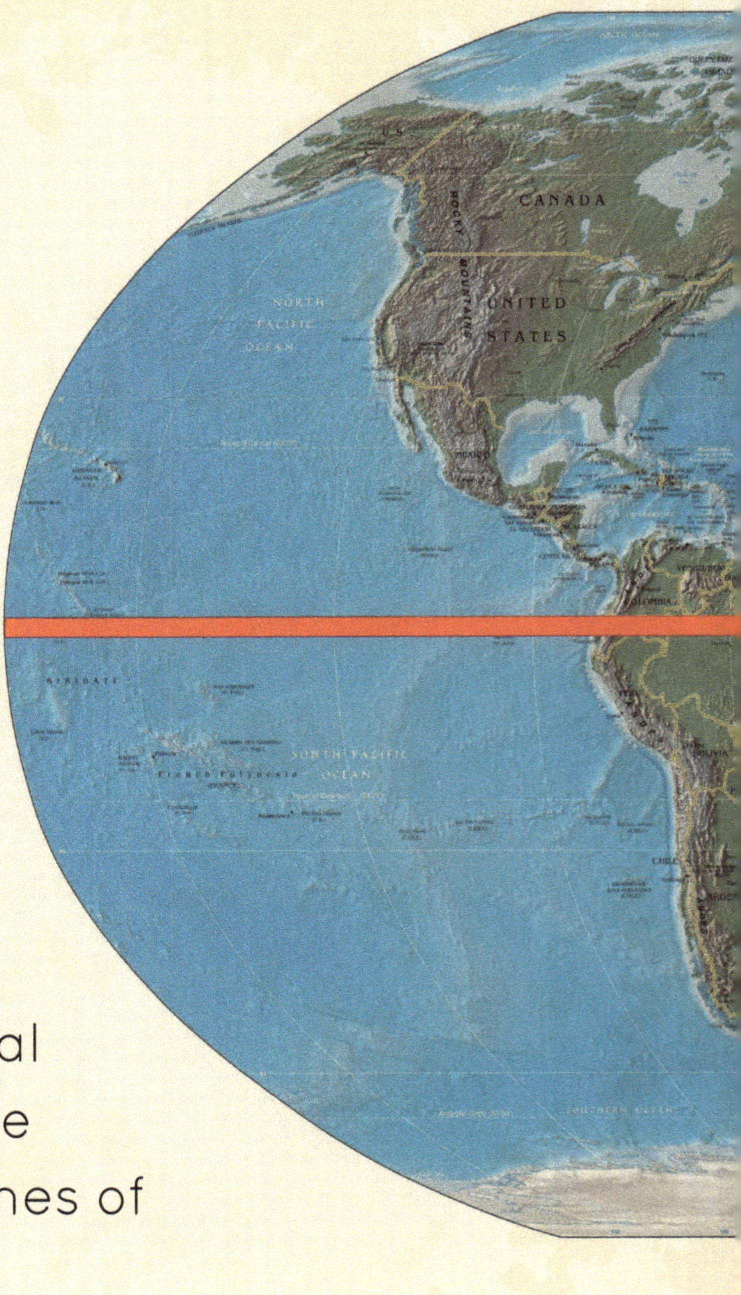

The equator is a line of latitude that is represented by 0 degrees, written with symbols as 0°. The lines running parallel to the equator are the horizontal lines of latitude. There are exactly 180 degrees or lines of latitude.

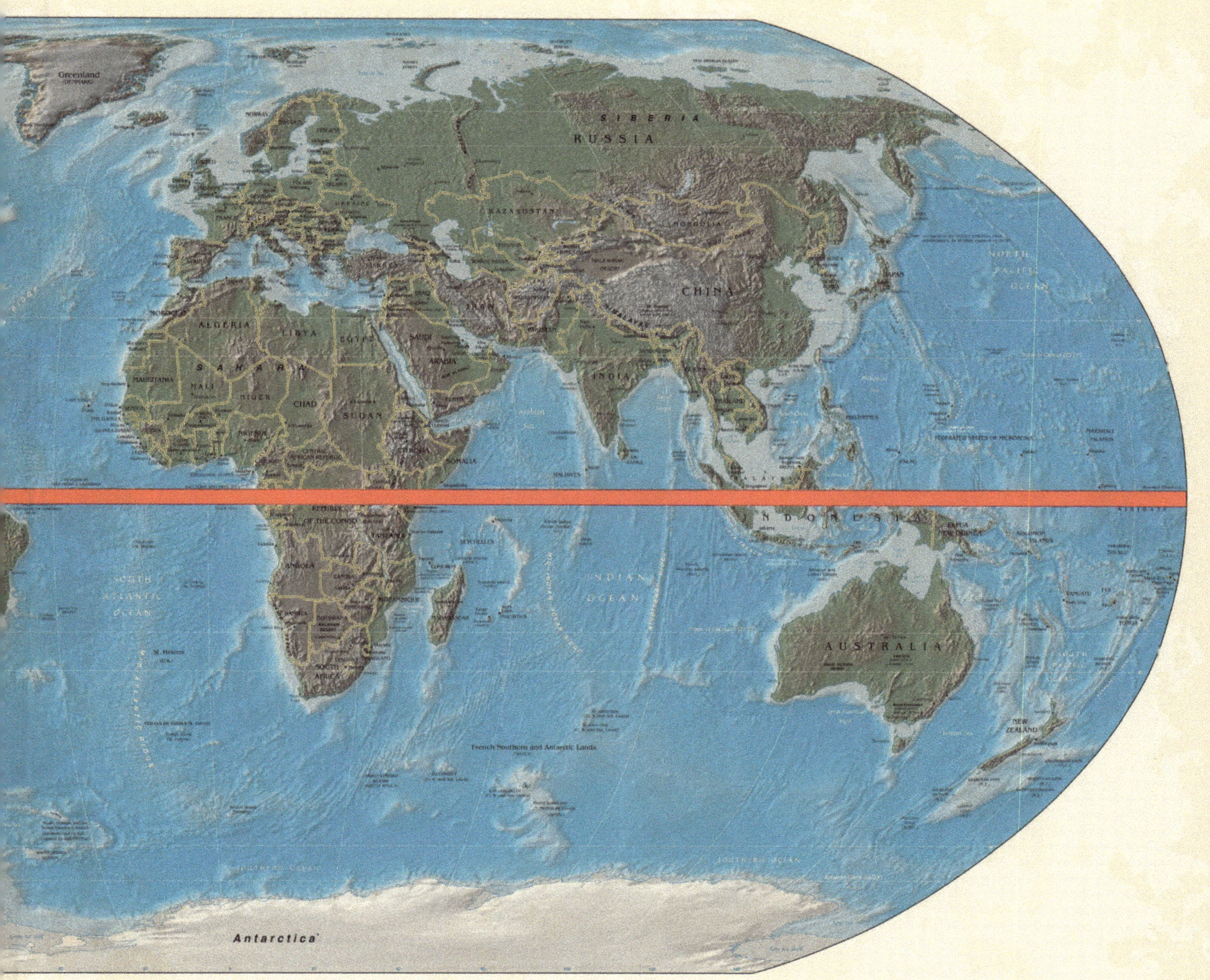



## WORLD MAP WITH EQUATOR

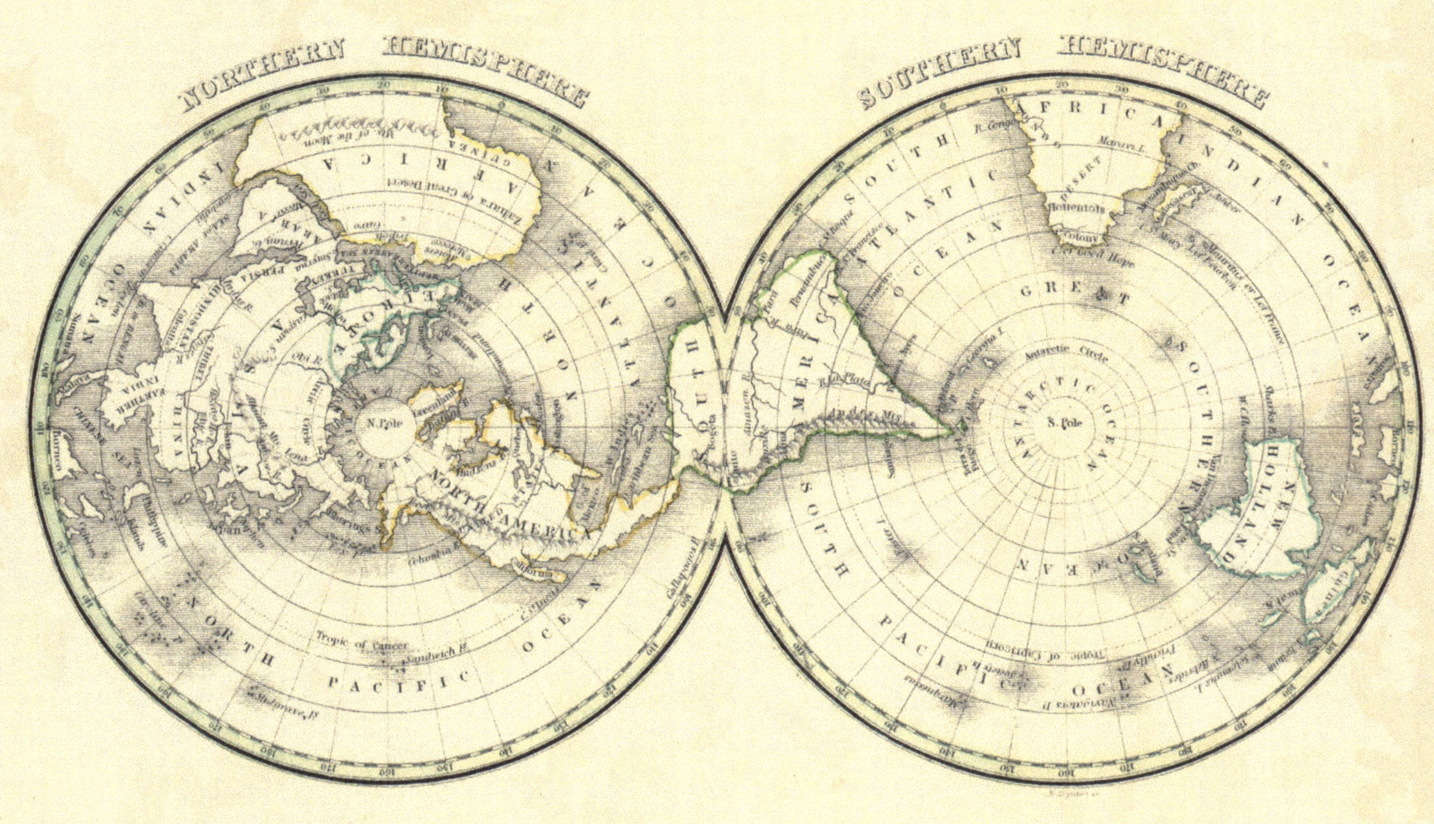


# 1838 BRADFORD MAP OF THE WORLD
## ON POLAR PROJECTION

The equator was an easy way to separate the Earth into a Northern and Southern Hemisphere, but to describe an Eastern and Western Hemisphere geographers needed to pick a starting point. They selected the location of Greenwich in the country of England. The line of longitude that travels through Greenwich is described as the Prime Meridian of 0 degrees of longitude.

Along with the Prime Meridian, the line of longitude on Earth's opposite side at the 180-degree position, divides the Earth into Eastern and Western Hemispheres.

There are 360 lines or degrees of longitude. Longitude specifies time zones, but both latitude and longitude are necessary to pinpoint locations.

# CLIMATE AND HEMISPHERES

The seasonal tilt of Earth, either toward the Sun or away from it, gives us the change in seasons. In the Northern Hemisphere, the summer months are from the month of June through the month of September. When people in the Northern Hemisphere are experiencing winter, those in the Southern Hemisphere are experiencing summer, beginning in December and ending in March.

EARTH'S NORTHERN HEMISPHERE
WITH SEA ICE AND CLOUDS

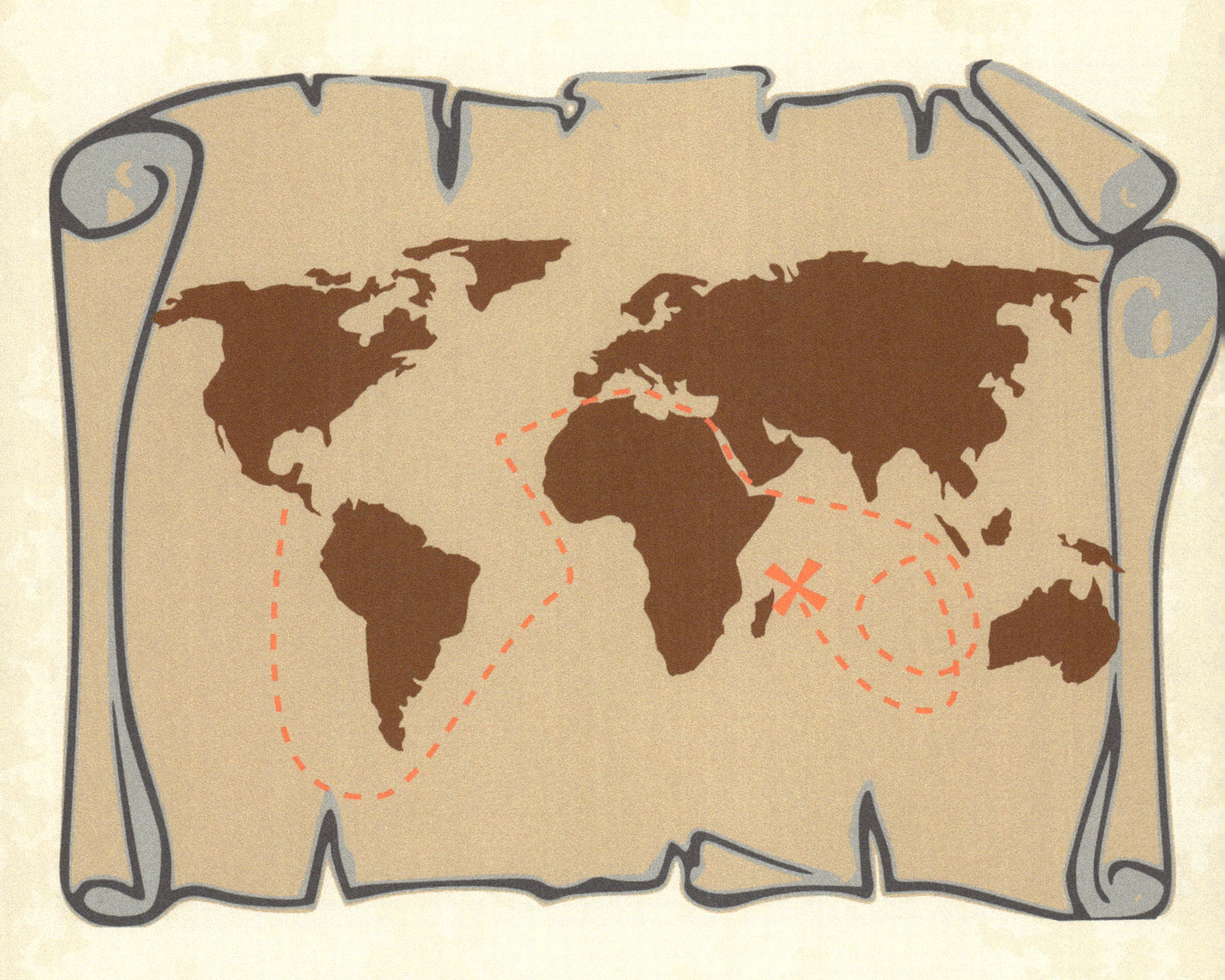

# TYPES OF MAPS

There are many different types of maps that geographers, other scientists, and scholars use. Maps are available in both print and digital form. Digital maps are available on mobile devices. Here are some of the more common types of maps:

These types of maps show the physical characteristics of a place such as mountains and lakes.

Waterways are depicted using blue. The color green is used for elevations that are lower, and brown is used for higher elevations.

These types of maps also depict physical features. However, instead of using colors for elevations, curved lines are used. These lines, which are called contour lines, show the changes in elevation by 100-foot increments. When the lines are close together, it means the terrain is very steep. When they are far apart, it means the terrain is somewhat flat.

A
Topographical Map
OF THE
WHITE MOUNTAINS,
OF
NEW HAMPSHIRE.
By C. H. Hitchcock.
OSGOOD'S
WHITE MOUNTAIN
GUIDE BOOK.
SCALE, 3 MILES TO AN INCH. (½ size of model)

Lisbon
Algiers
Tunis
Athens
Nicosia
Teheran
Rabat
MOROCCO
TUNISIA
Valetta
Tripoli
Beirut
Damascus
Baghdad
Jerusalem
Amman
Kuwait
ALGERIA
LIBYA
Cairo
EGYPT
Riyadh
Manama
Doha
WESTERN SAHARA
MAURITANIA
MALI
NIGER
SUDAN
ERITREA
Sanaa
CAPE VERDE
Nouakchott
Asamara
Praia
Dakar
SENEGAL
CHAD
Ndjamena
DJIBOUTI
Banjul
GAMBIA
Niamey
Ouagadougou
SOMALILAND (disputed)
Bissau
BURKINA FASO
NIGERIA
Abuja
Addis Ababa
Hargeysa
GUINEA-BISSAU
GUINEA
Conakry
CÔTE D'IVOIRE
GHANA
TOGO
BENIN
CAMEROON
CENTRAL AFRICAN REPUBLIC
Bangui
SOUTH SUDAN
ETHIOPIA
SOMALIA
Freetown
SIERRA LEONE
Yamoussoukro
Accra
Lome
Cotonou
Yaounde
Mogadishu
LIBERIA
Monrovia
Abidjan
Malabo
EQUATORIAL GUINEA
Sao Tome
Libreville
GABON
CONGO
UGANDA
Kampala
KENYA
Nairobi
SAO TOMÉ AND PRÍNCIPE
DR CONGO
RWANDA
Kigali
Brazzaville
Kinshasa
Bujumbura
BURUNDI
TANZANIA
Dar es Salaam
Luanda
ANGOLA
COMOROS
Moroni
ZAMBIA
MALAWI
Lilongwe
MOZAMBIQUE
Lusaka
Harare
MADAGASCAR
Antananarivo
ZIMBABWE
NAMIBIA
BOTSWANA
Windhoek
Gaborone
Pretoria
Maputo
Mbabane
SWAZILAND
Bloemfontein
Maseru
LESOTHO
SOUTH AFRICA

# POLITICAL MAP

A political map shows the boundaries of states and nations. For example, a map of the United States showing the state borders, as well as the borders with the countries of Canada and Mexico, would be a political map.

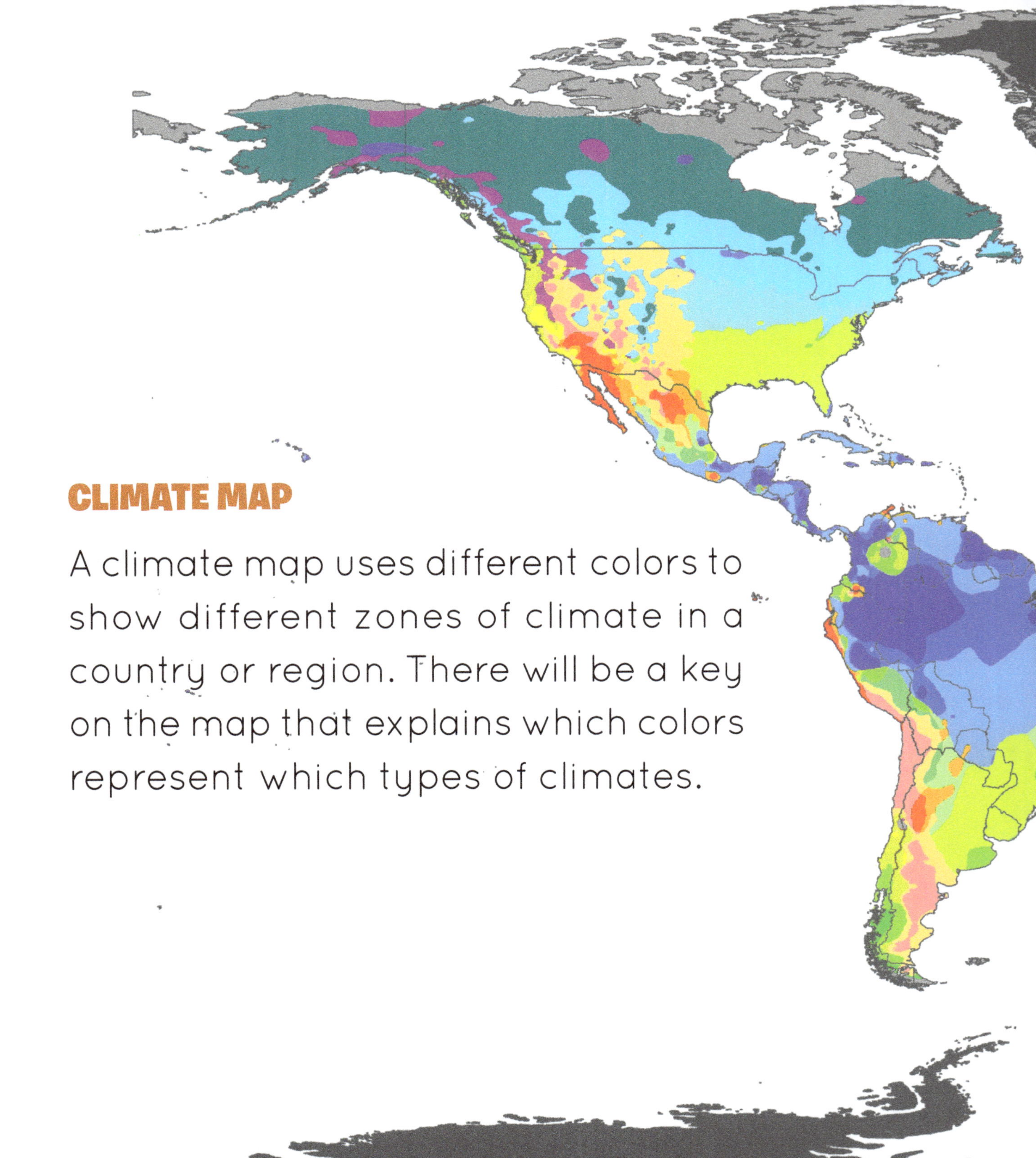

## CLIMATE MAP

A climate map uses different colors to show different zones of climate in a country or region. There will be a key on the map that explains which colors represent which types of climates.

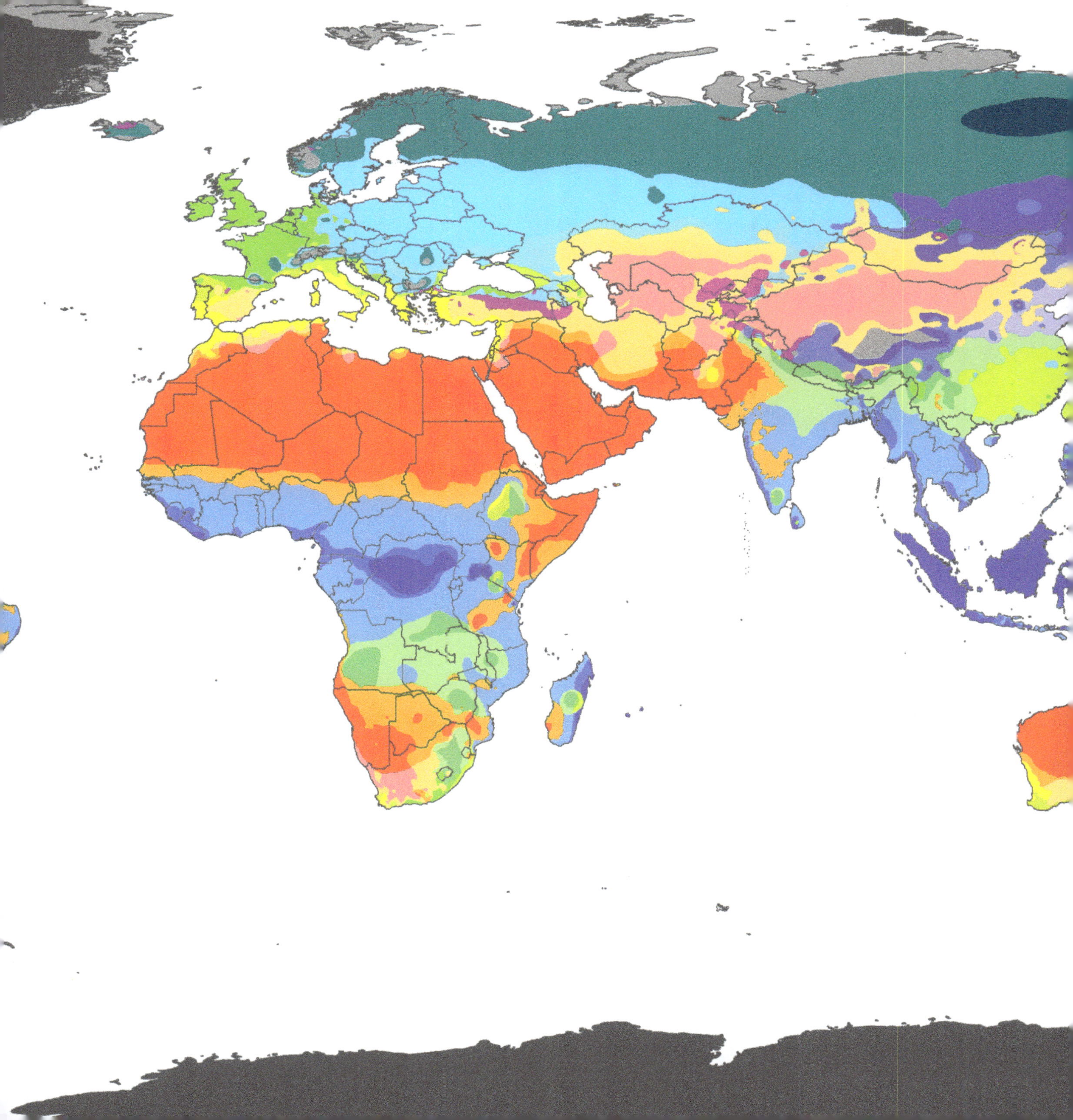

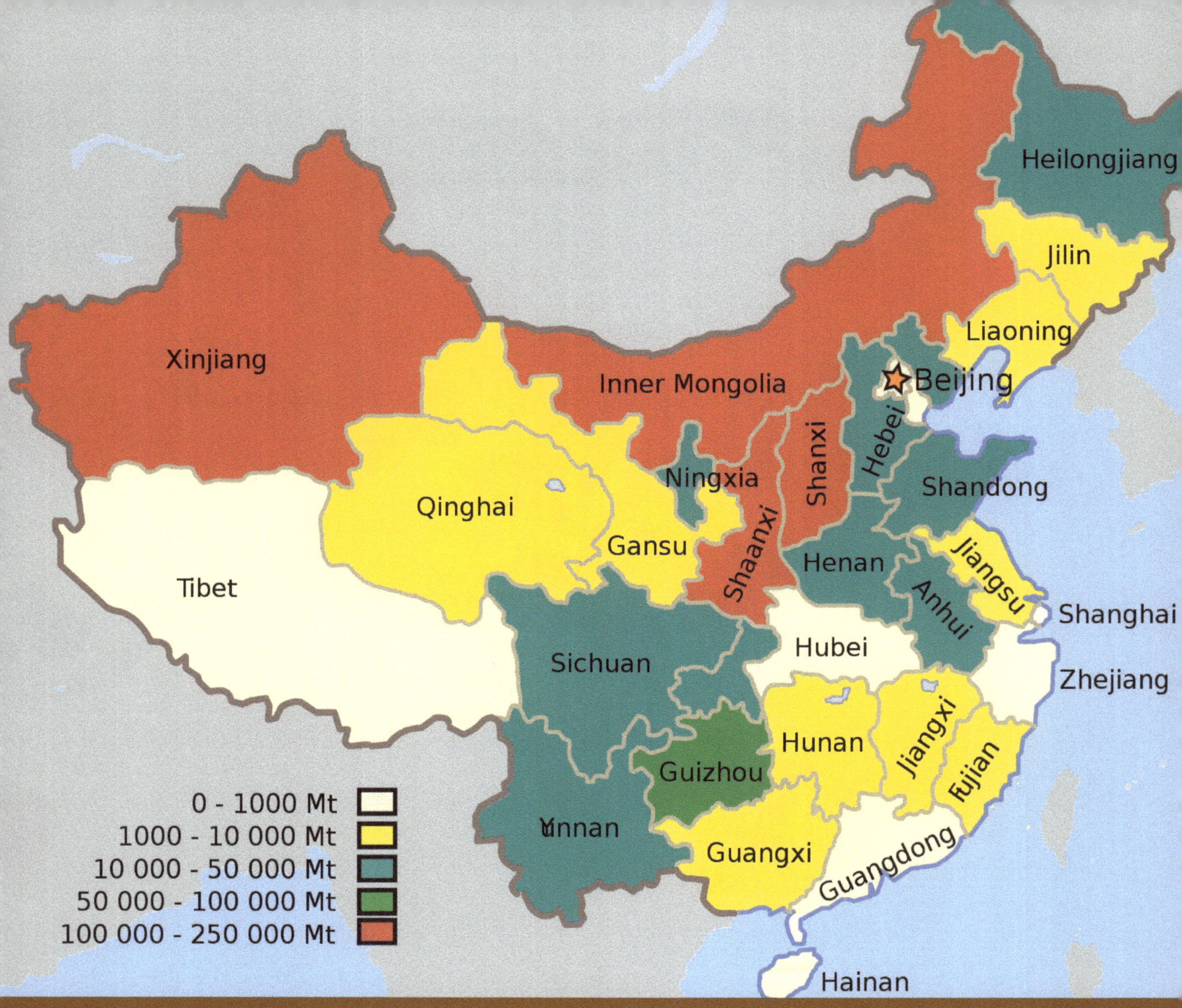

Heilongjiang
Jilin
Liaoning
Xinjiang
Inner Mongolia
Beijing
Shanxi
Hebei
Shandong
Ningxia
Qinghai
Shaanxi
Gansu
Henan
Jiangsu
Anhui
Shanghai
Tibet
Hubei
Zhejiang
Sichuan
Hunan
Jiangxi
Fujian
Guizhou
Yunnan
Guangxi
Guangdong
Hainan
0 - 1000 Mt
1000 - 10 000 Mt
10 000 - 50 000 Mt
50 000 - 100 000 Mt
100 000 - 250 000 Mt
MAP OF CHINA COAL RESOURCES

## ECONOMIC OR RESOURCE MAP

This type of map uses different symbols to represent agricultural products, natural resources, or energy sources. Once again, there will be a key or legend on the map that tells what the different symbols signify.

## ROAD MAP

This is the type of map that many everyday people use to get from place to place. It shows highways, roads, airports, locations of cities, and places of interest. Interstate highways are depicted with wider lines than the state highways.

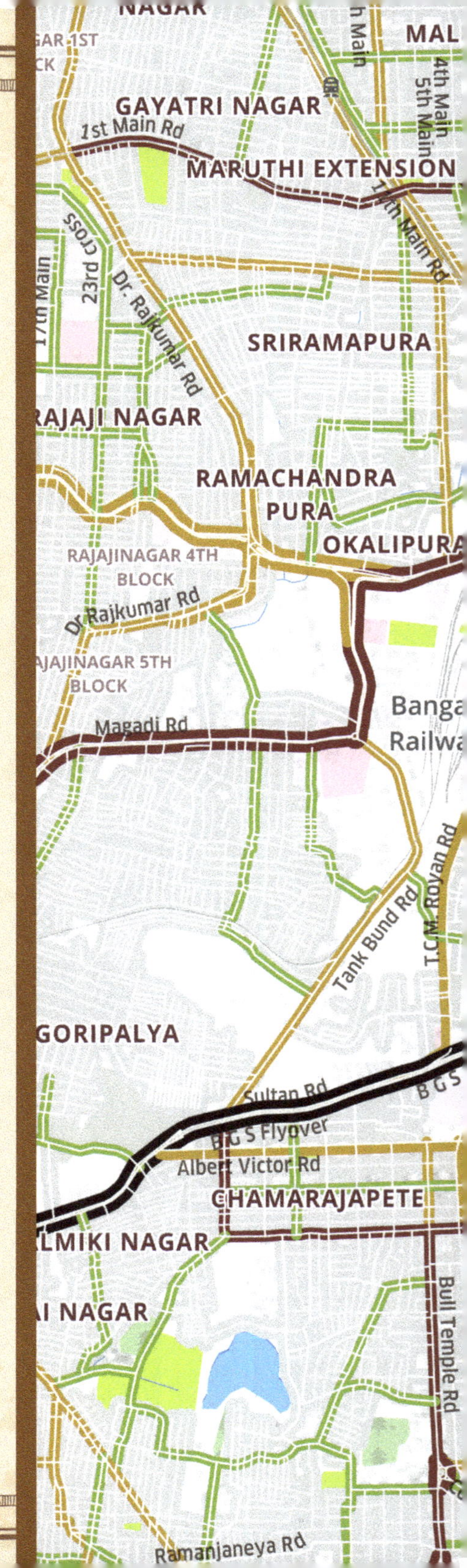

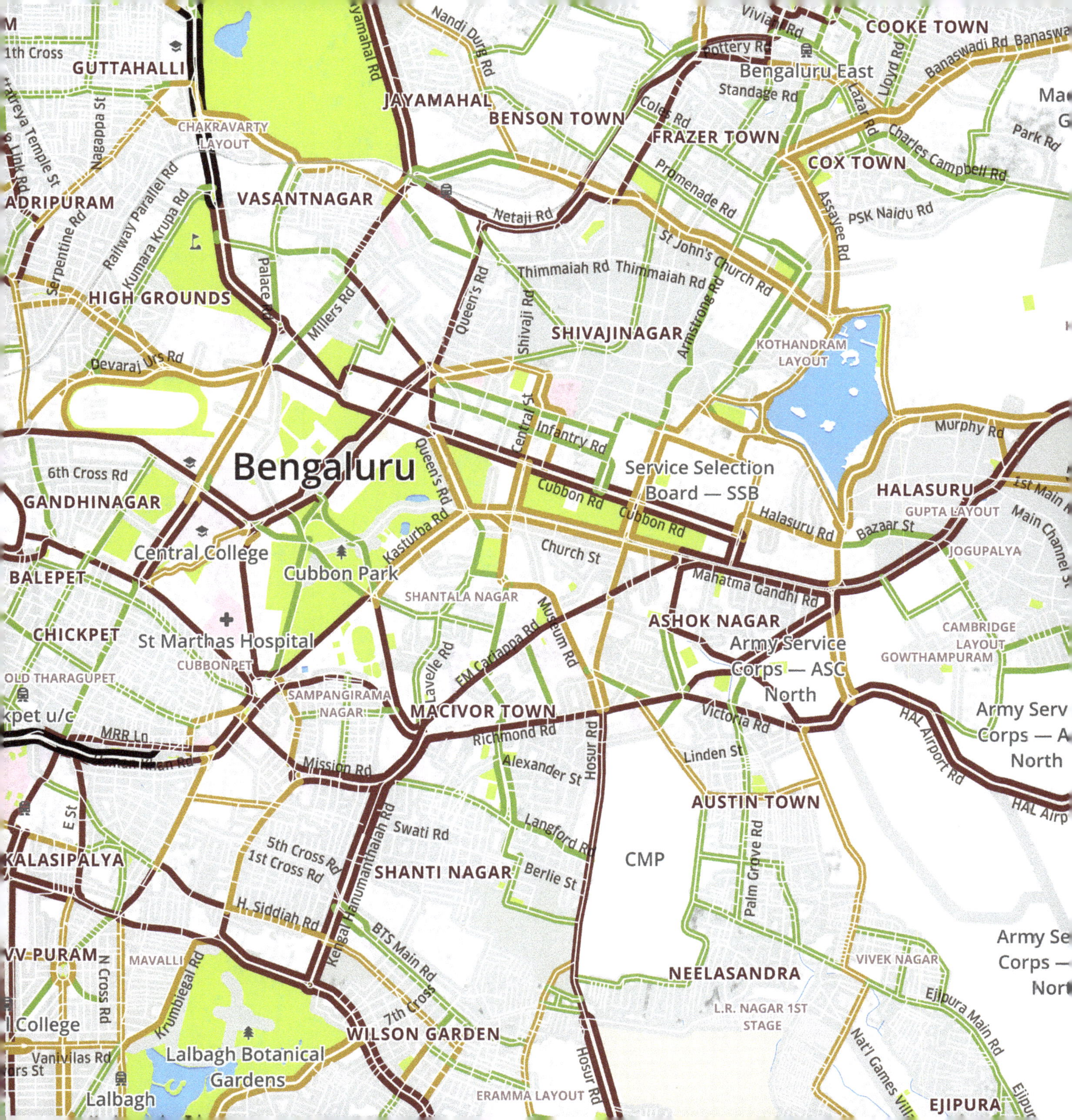
11th Cross
GUTTAHALLI
CHAKRAVARTY LAYOUT
JAYAMAHAL
BENSON TOWN
Nandi Durg Rd
Coles Rd
Standage Rd
Bengaluru East
COOKE TOWN
Banaswadi Rd
Banaswadi
Viviani Rd
Lottery Rd
FRAZER TOWN
COX TOWN
Lazar Rd
Lloyd Rd
Charles Campbell Rd
Park Rd
PSK Naidu Rd
ADRIPURAM
VASANTNAGAR
Promenade Rd
Netaji Rd
Assavee Rd
Railway Parallel Rd
Kumara Krupa Rd
Serpentine Rd
Nagappa St
Link Rd
Atreya Temple St
HIGH GROUNDS
Palace Rd
Millers Rd
Queen's Rd
Thimmaiah Rd
Thimmaiah Rd
St John's Church Rd
Armstrong Rd
Shivaji Rd
SHIVAJINAGAR
KOTHANDRAM LAYOUT
Murphy Rd
Devaraj Urs Rd
Central St
Infantry Rd
Queen's Rd
Bengaluru
Service Selection Board — SSB
HALASURU
1st Main Rd
GUPTA LAYOUT
Main Channel St
6th Cross Rd
GANDHINAGAR
Cubbon Rd
Cubbon Rd
Halasuru Rd
Bazaar St
JOGUPALYA
Central College
Kasturba Rd
Church St
Mahatma Gandhi Rd
Cubbon Park
SHANTALA NAGAR
ASHOK NAGAR
CAMBRIDGE LAYOUT
GOWTHAMPURAM
BALEPET
St Marthas Hospital
Army Service Corps — ASC North
CHICKPET
CUBBONPET
Museum Rd
Lavelle Rd
EM Cariappa Rd
OLD THARAGUPET
SAMPANGIRAMA NAGAR
MACIVOR TOWN
Victoria Rd
Army Serv Corps — A North
kpet u/c
MRR Ln
Richmond Rd
Hosur Rd
Linden St
HAL Airport Rd
Mission Rd
Alexander St
AUSTIN TOWN
HAL Airp
KALASIPALYA
E St
5th Cross Rd
1st Cross Rd
Swati Rd
Langford Rd
Berlie St
CMP
Palm Grove Rd
SHANTI NAGAR
H. Siddiah Rd
BTS Main Rd
Kengal Hanumanthaiah Rd
VV PURAM
N Cross Rd
MAVALLI
Krumbiegal Rd
7th Cross
WILSON GARDEN
VIVEK NAGAR
NEELASANDRA
Army Se Corps — Nort
College
L.R. NAGAR 1ST STAGE
Ejipura Main Rd
Vanivilas Rd
Lalbagh Botanical Gardens
Lalbagh
ERAMMA LAYOUT
Hosur Rd
Nat'l Games Vill
EJIPURA

# Injury mortality rate (per 100,000 population), 2008

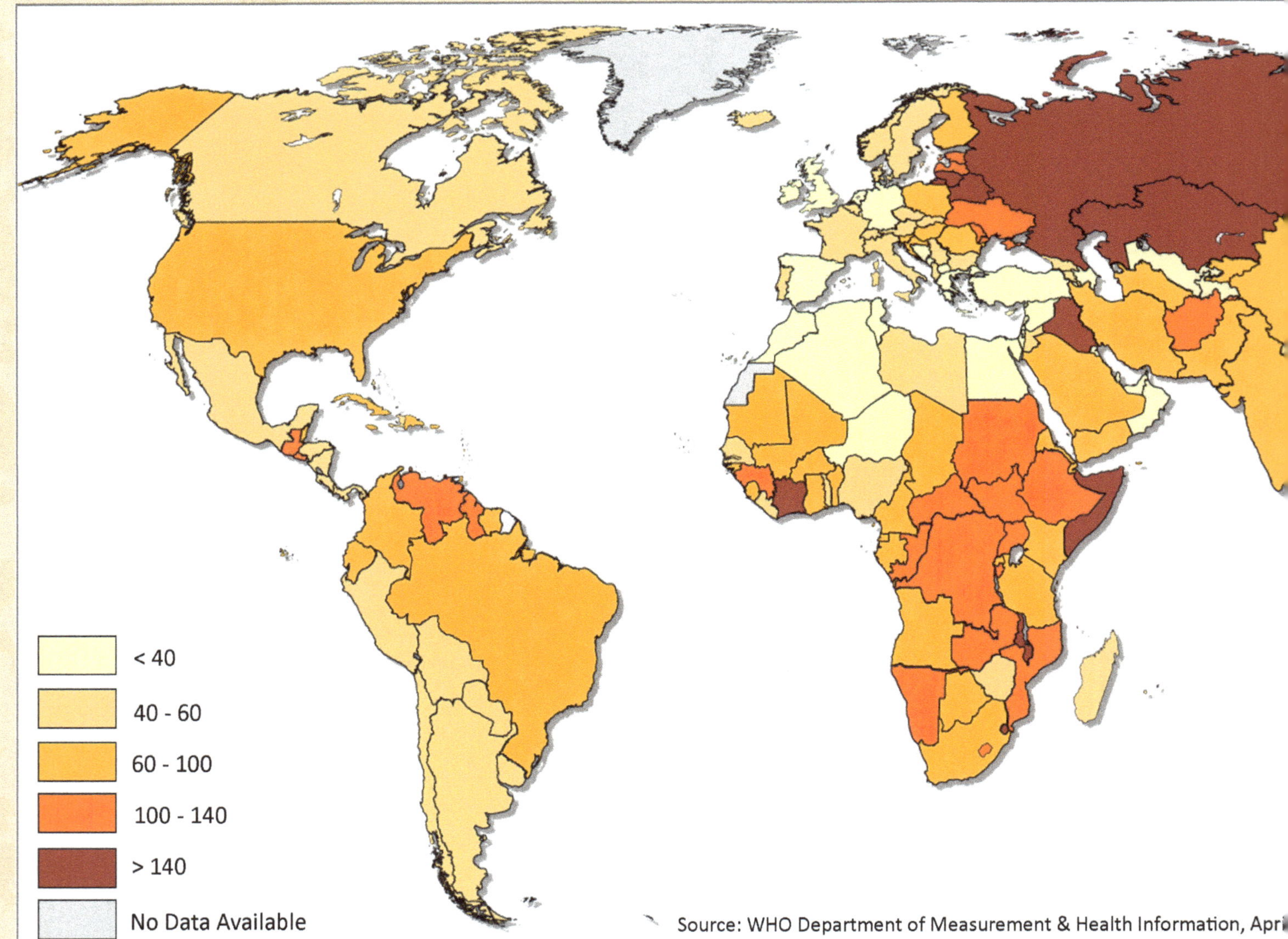

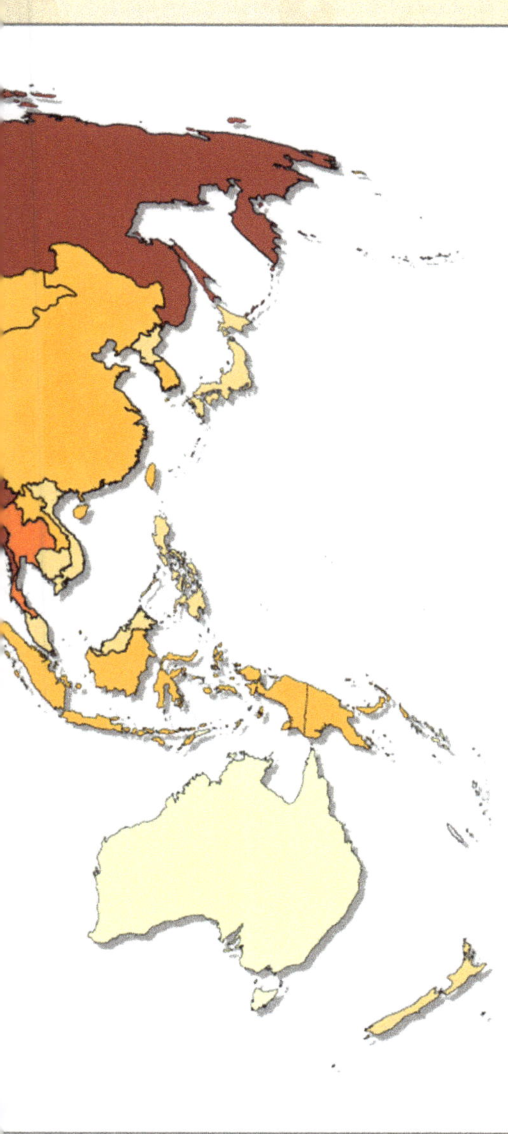

## THEMATIC MAP

Thematic maps are becoming more popular and more common. They are based on a specific set of data. For example, a map could show the spread of a disease throughout a region, or the average snowfall for a specific location, or the change in population over time in a designated area. As more and more data is becoming collected, there will be new types of maps to give quick visual snapshots of the information in a way that is easy to use.

# GEOGRAPHIC REGIONS

Geographers frequently talk about geographic regions. Regions are specified by a certain physical or cultural characteristic. For example, the Amazon Basin, which is located in South America, is a physical region associated with the Amazon River and its tributaries.

Atlantic Ocean
Pacific Ocean
VENEZUELA
Caracas
COLOMBIA
Bogotá
GUYANA
Georgetown
Quito
ECUADOR
Macapá
Belém
Para
Jari
Paru
Trombetas
Branco
Negro
Vaupés
Apaporis
Caquetá
Japurá
Putumayo
Napo
Tigre
Pastaza
Marañón
Iquitos
Huallaga
Ucayali
Javary
Juruá
Purus
Madeira
Manaus
Sanatarém
Imperatri
Tapajós
Iriri
Juruena
Teles Pires
Xingu
Araguaia
Tocantins
Machado
Arinos
Pucallpa
Rio Branco
Acre
Porto Velho
Tambo
Ene
Apurimac
Mantaro
Lima
PERU
Cusco
Madre de Dios
Beni
Mamoré
Guaporé
Grande
La Paz
Cochabamba
Santa Cruz
BOLIVIA
BRAZIL
Brasília
Rio de Janeiro
São Paulo

The Gobi Desert would be another region that is associated with a physical characteristic. The New York metropolitan region is a cultural region because it is associated with the population and culture of New York.

# READING MAPS

**T**he title of a map will give you clues as to what the mapmaker intended to depict on the map. Good quality maps have legends that explain the different symbols that are used on the map. For example, a square that has a flag positioned on the top of it generally represents a school.

Different types of roads are depicted with lines of various thicknesses and colors. Dashed lines sometimes represent borders.

UNITED KINGDOM
London
NETHERLANDS
The Hague
Calais
Lille
Brussels
BELGIUM
LUXEMBOURG
Frankfurt
English Channel
Dieppe
Amiens
Arras
Cherbourg
Le Havre
Rouen
Reims
Metz
GERMA
Caen
Versailles
Paris
Nancy
Strasbourg
Melun
Brest
St.-Brieuc
Troyes
Rennes
Le Mans
Mulhouse
Lorient
Orleans
Auxerre
Zürich
Angers
Tours
Dijon
Besancon
Nantes
Bourges
Nevers
Bern
Poitier
FRANCE
SWITZERLAND
La Rochelle
Vichy
Roanne
Geneva
Bay of
Limoges
Lyon
Annecy
Biscay
Clermont-Ferrand
Saint-Etienne
Brive
Milan
Bordeaux
Grenoble
ITA
Agen
Nimes
Nice
Toulouse
Montpellier
Aix-en-Provence
MONACO
Biarritz
Beziers
Marseille
Toulon
Bilbao
Tarbes
Perpignan
Bastia

# However, symbols on maps published in the United States may represent something different in other countries.

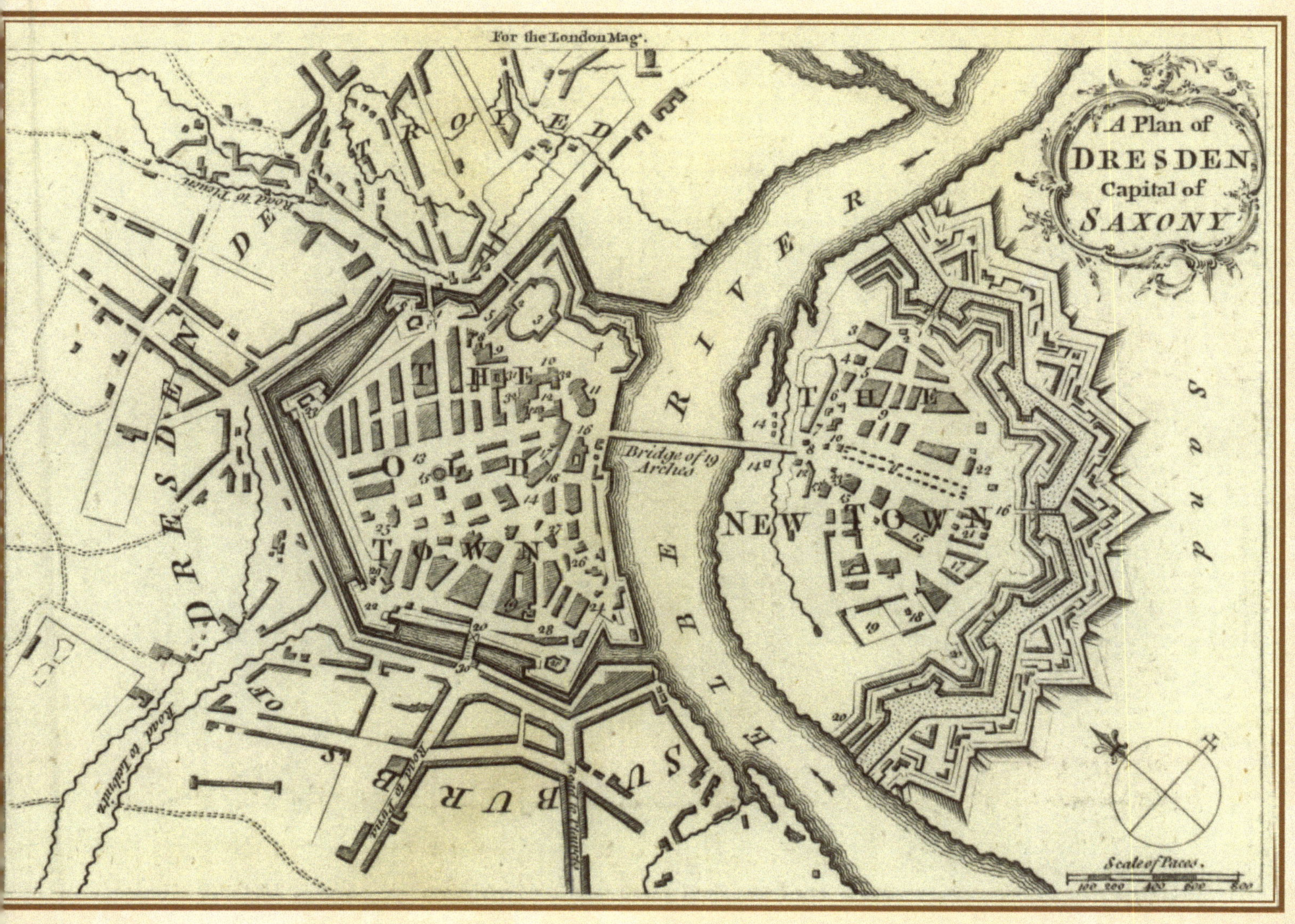

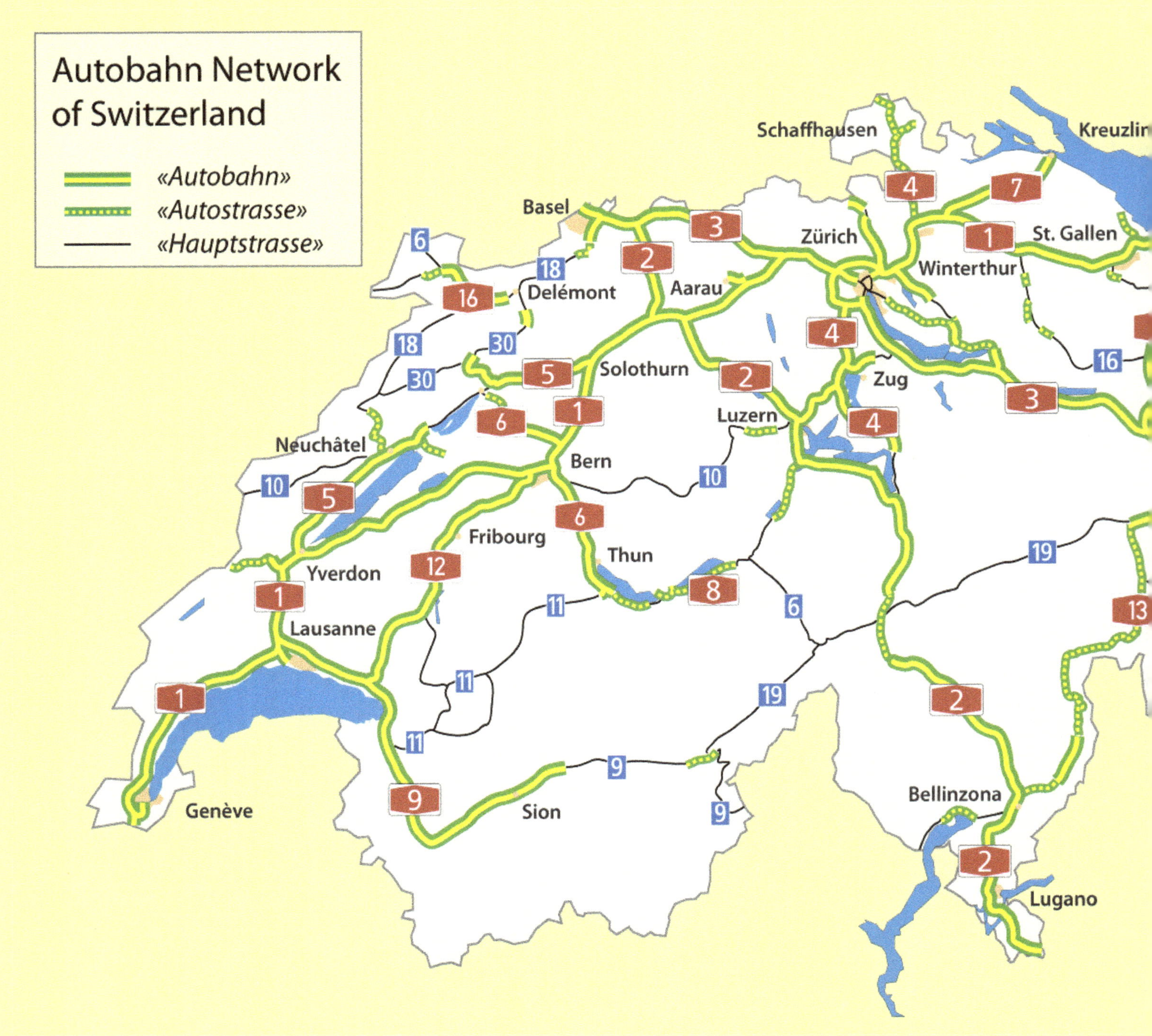

Autobahn Network
of Switzerland
«Autobahn»
«Autostrasse»
«Hauptstrasse»
Schaffhausen
Kreuzlin
Basel
4
7
3
2
1
Zürich
St. Gallen
Aarau
Winterthur
6
18
16
Delémont
4
18
30
5
Solothurn
2
16
30
1
Zug
3
6
Luzern
Neuchâtel
4
10
5
6
Bern
10
Fribourg
19
12
Thun
Yverdon
11
8
1
6
Lausanne
11
13
1
11
19
2
9
1
11
19
9
9
Bellinzona
9
Sion
Genève
2
Lugano

For example, on a Swiss map the symbol used for a railroad is the same symbol used on some topographical maps for secondary highways in the United States. Make sure you study the key or legend so you know what the symbols mean.

A map should have an arrow that designates which way is north. Some topographic maps point to the North Pole as true north and also to where your compass directs, which is magnetic north in the northern regions of Canada.

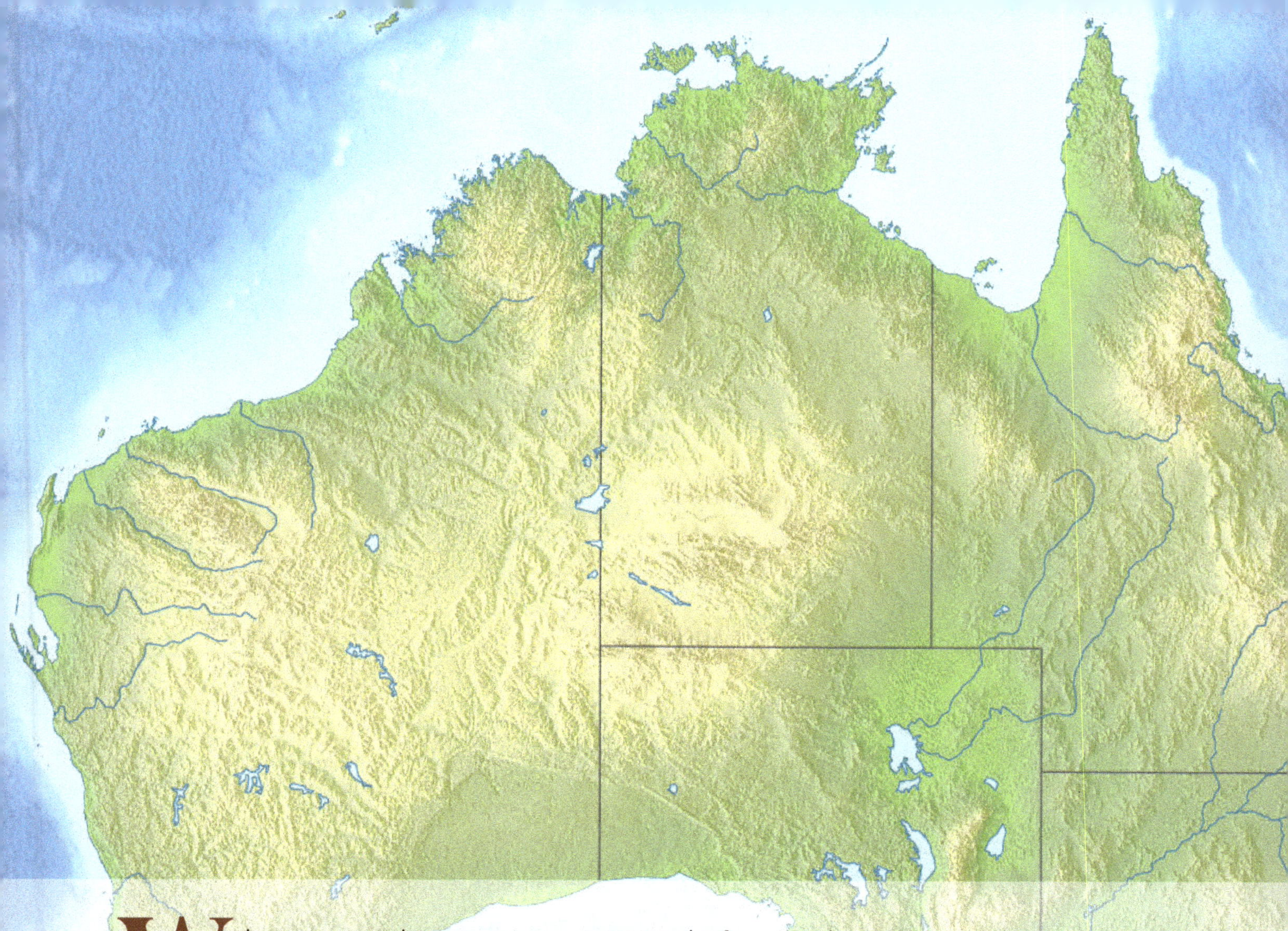

When colors are used for elevation, some people misinterpret it. For example, green is used for lower elevations on physical maps, but we associate green with a fertile farm area when it might be a low-lying desert.

# SUMMARY

Geography is the study of the physical features of the Earth. It's also the study of how people use the Earth's resources and interact with all the elements in their environment including other people, plants and animals, and non-living natural resources like soil and water. Geographers make frequent use of globes and different types of maps as they research and make recommendations.

INDIANA
OHIO
KENTUCKY
TENN.
MISS.
ALABAMA
GEORGIA
FLORIDA
LOUISIANA
SOUTH CAROLINA
NORTH CAROLINA
VIRGINIA
Wash. D.C.
MD.
W. VA.
Columbus
Frankfort
Nashville
Knoxville
Chattanooga
Greenville
Memphis
Birmingham
Montgomery
Jackson
Atlanta
Tallahassee
Tampa
Sarasota
Pensacola
Mobile
New Orleans
Jacksonville
Daytona Beach
C. Canaveral
Orlando
Miami
Key West
Everglades
Savannah
Charleston
Columbia
Charlotte
Raleigh
Richmond
Norfolk
Detroit
Toledo
Dayton
Columbus
Cincinnati
Charleston
Pittsburgh
GULF OF MEXICO
YUCATAN
Gulf of Campeche
Mérida
Valladolid
Yucatan Channel
Havana
CUBA
Campeche
Veracruz
Tampico
Matamoros
BELIZE
Cozumel

MANITOBA
SASKATCHEWAN
ONTARIO
QUÉBEC
Fort George
Winnipeg
Lake Superior
Lake Huron
Ottawa
Montreal
Toronto
Lake Ontario
MONTANA
NORTH DAKOTA
Bismarck
St Paul
MINNESOTA
WISCONSIN
MICHIGAN
Lake Michigan
Detroit
Lake Erie
VT MAINE
NEW HAMPSHIRE
MASSACHUSETTS
RI
CONNECTICUT
NEW YORK
New York
NEW JERSEY
OREGON
IDAHO
WYOMING
SOUTH DAKOTA
IOWA
Omaha
Chicago
ILLINOIS
INDIANA
OHIO
PENNSYLVANIA
MARYLAND
DELAWARE
NEVADA
Salt Lake City
UTAH
NEBRASKA
Denver
COLORADO
KANSAS
MISSOURI
KENTUCKY
WEST VIRGINIA
VIRGINIA
Washington D.C.
UNITED STATES
Las Vegas
ARIZONA
NEW MEXICO
OKLAHOMA
ARKANSAS
TENNESSEE
Atlanta
NORTH CAROLINA
SOUTH CAROLINA
Phoenix
Tucson
Fort Worth
Dallas
MISSISSIPPI
ALABAMA
GEORGIA
Hamilton
Juarez
El Paso
TEXAS
LOUISIANA
Mobile
Jacksonville
Bermuda
(UK)
Houston
New Orleans
Chihuahua
FLORIDA
Monterrey
GULF OF
MEXICO
Miami
BAHAMAS
Turks & Caicos Islands
(UK)
Mazatlan
Havana
Greater Antilles
PUERTO RICO
San Luis Potosi
CUBA
Virgin Islands
MEXICO
Merida
Cayman Islands
(UK)
HAITI
DOMINICAN
REPUBLIC
JAMAICA
Mexico City
Veracruz
BELIZE
Juchitan
HONDURAS
CARIBBEAN SEA
GUATEMALA
Tegucigalpa
EL SALVADOR
NICARAGUA
Panama

Awesome! Now that you've read all about the study of Geography, you may want to read about time and climate zones in the Baby Professor book World Geography–Time & Climates Zones–Latitude, Longitude, Tropics, Meridian and More | Geography for Kids.

Visit

# www.BabyProfessorBooks.com

to download Free Baby Professor eBooks
and view our catalog of new and exciting
Children's Books